My Dad Had ?

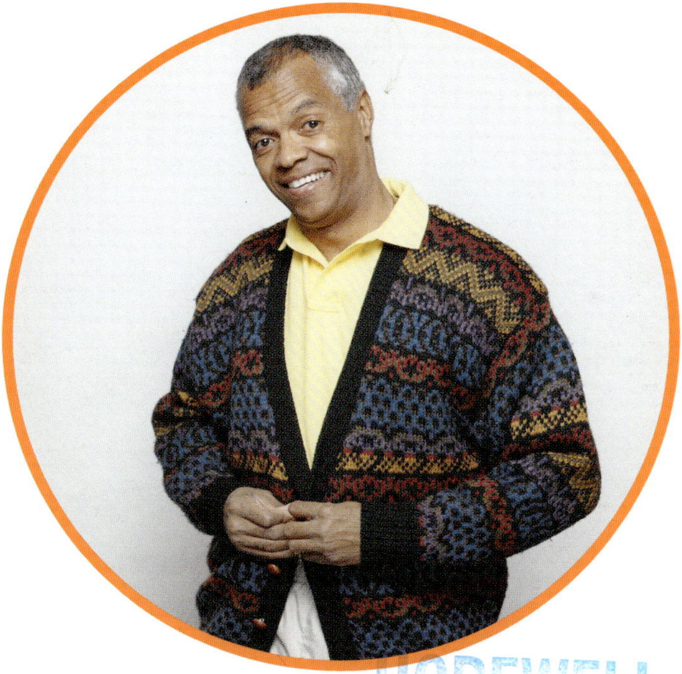

by Cathy French

My dad had 1 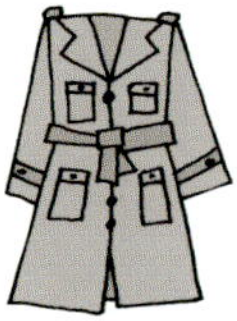 .

coat

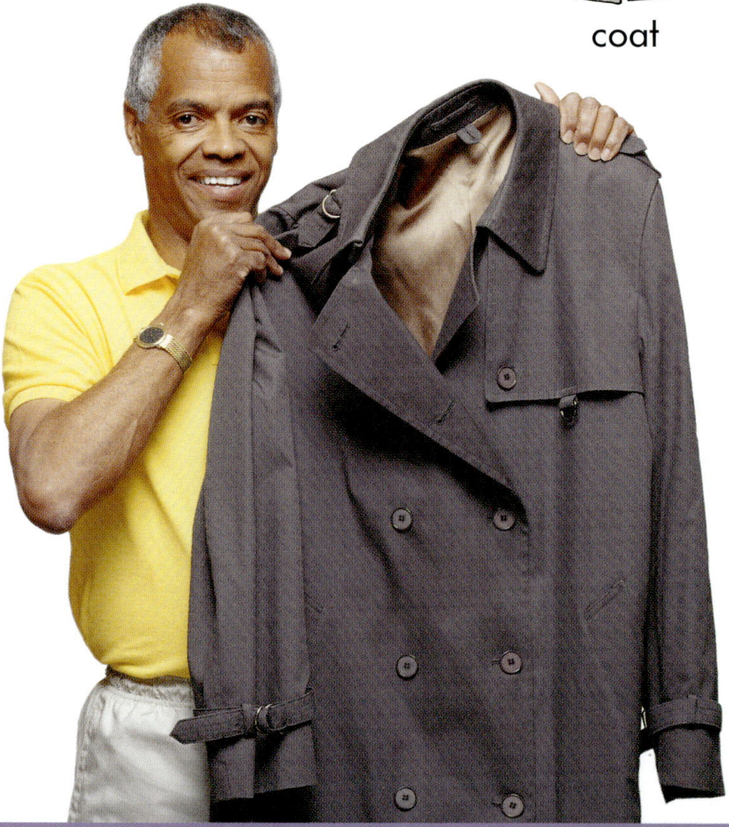

My dad had

2 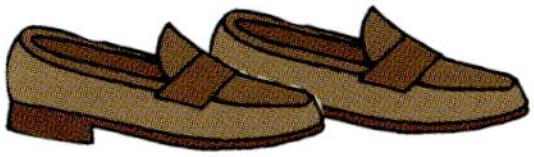 .

shoes

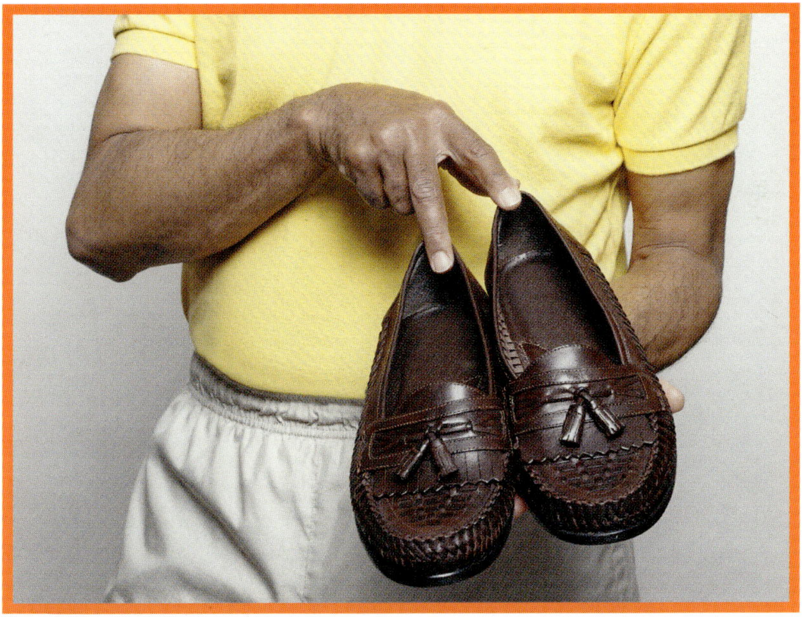

My dad had

4 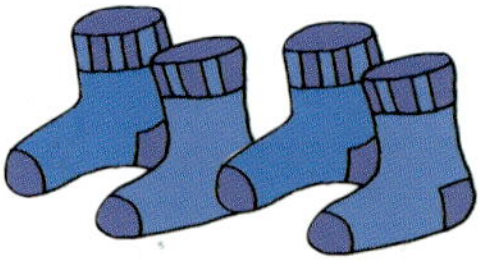 .

socks

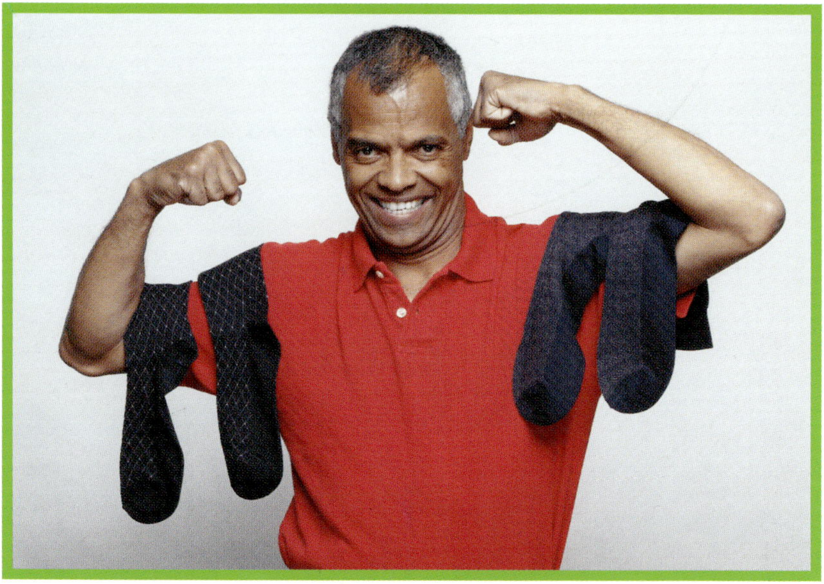

My dad had

2 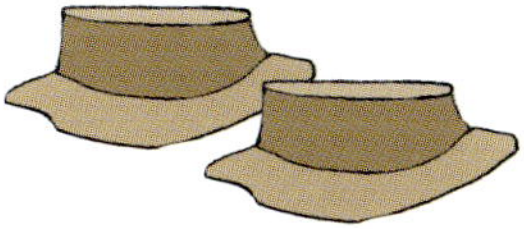 .

hats

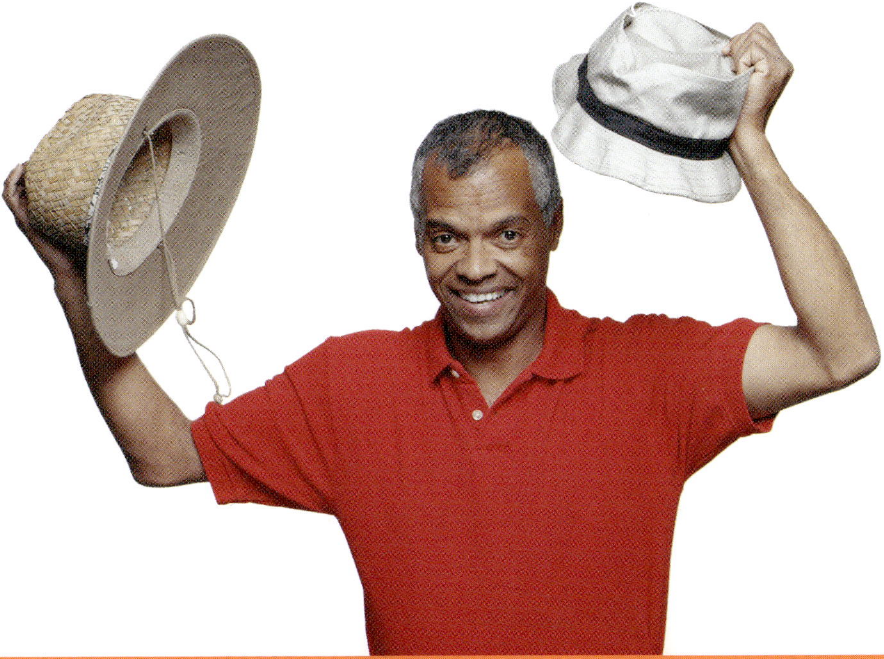

My dad had

5 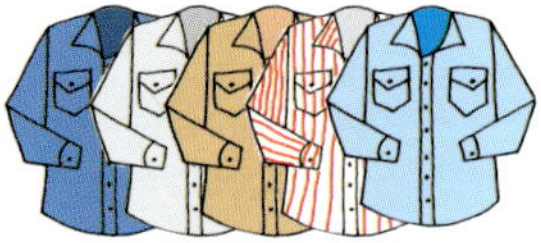 .

shirts

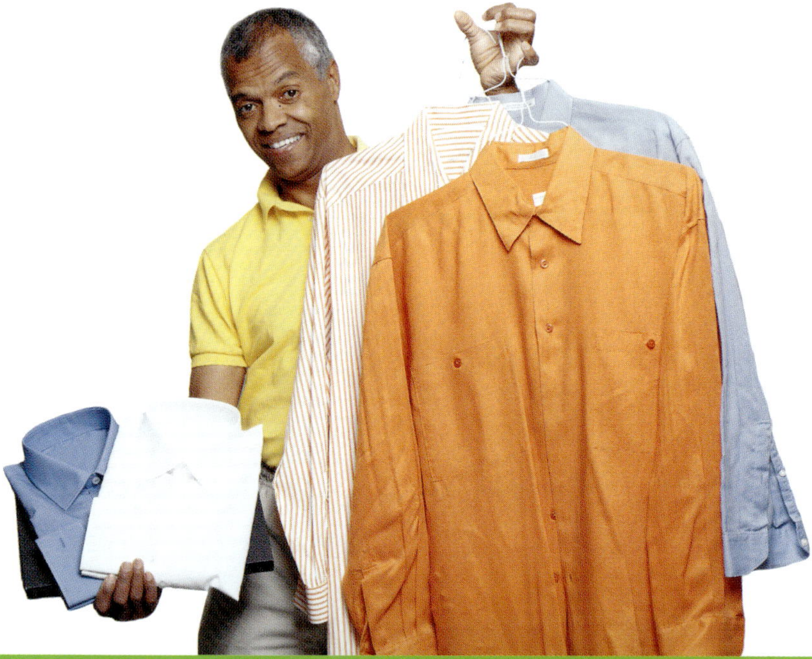

My dad had 3 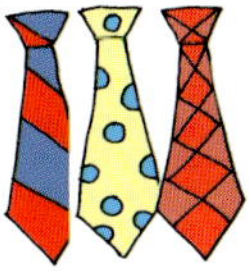 .

ties

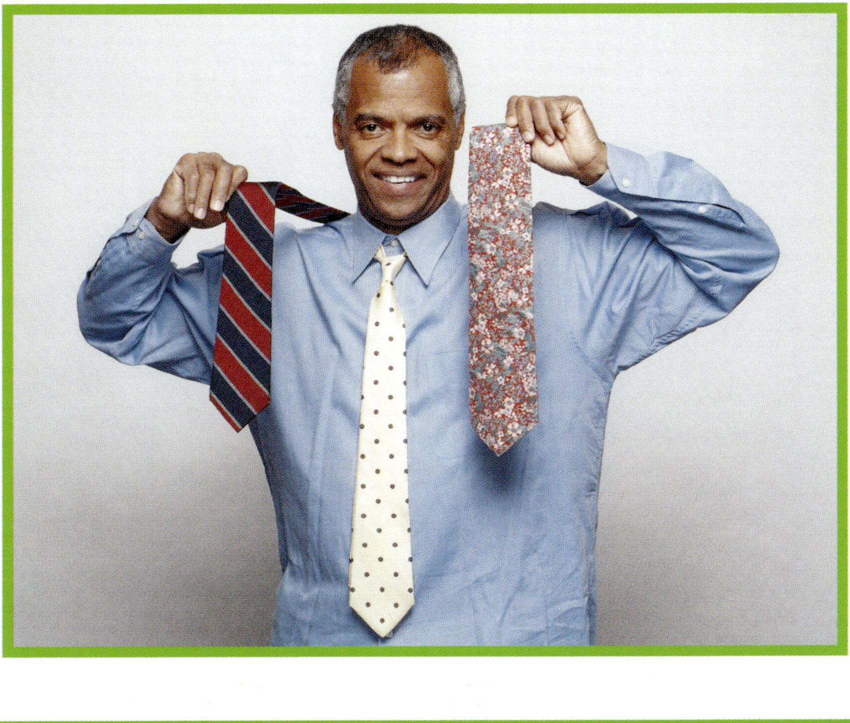

My dad had 4 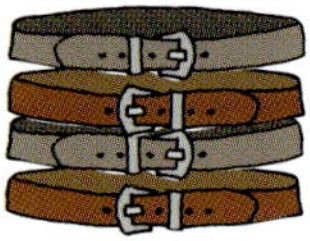 .

belts

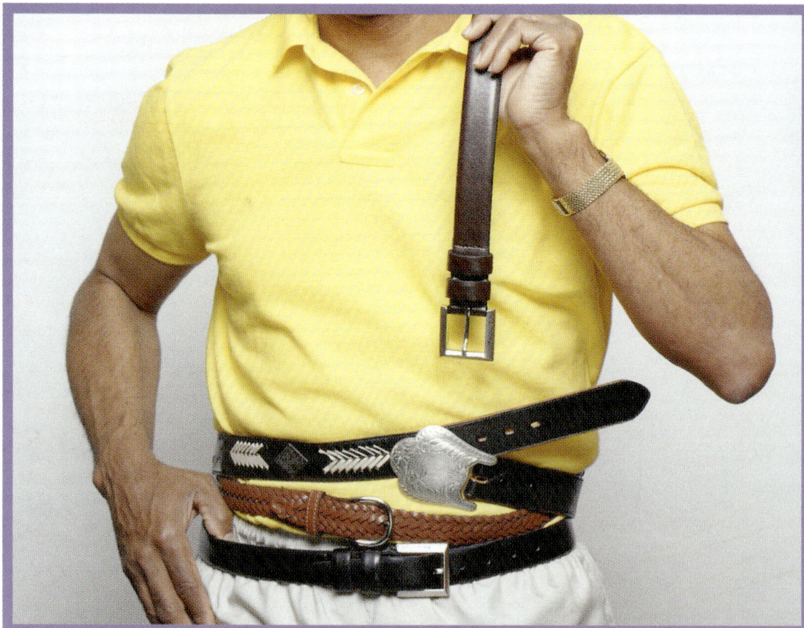